INSPIRATION FOR ARTISTS

EMILY DARCY

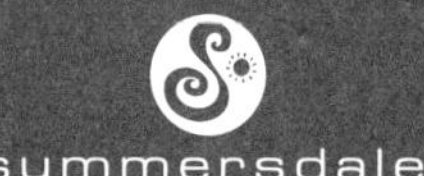

INSPIRATION FOR ARTISTS

First published in 2012

Summersdale Publishers Ltd
46 West Street
Chichester
West Sussex
PO19 1RP
UK

www.summersdale.com

Printed and bound in the Czech Republic

ISBN: 978-1-78685-056-0

To......................................

From..................................

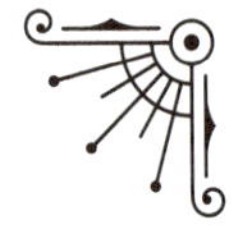

To be an artist, you have to give up everything, including the desire to be a good artist.

Jasper Johns

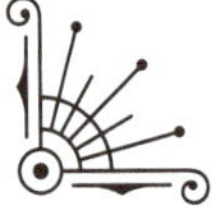

CREATIVITY TAKES COURAGE.

Henri Matisse

I don't think art is propaganda;
it should be something
that liberates your soul.

Keith Haring

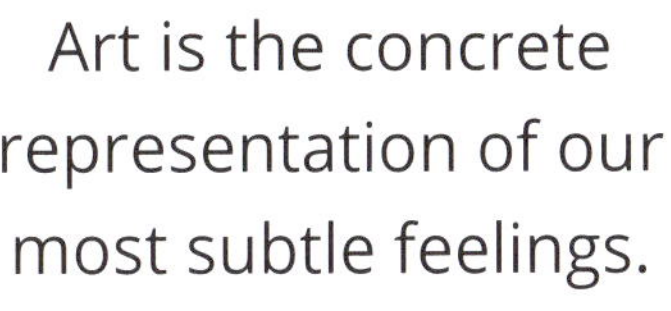

Art is the concrete representation of our most subtle feelings.

Agnes Martin

CREATING IS ABOUT TRUSTING THE PROCESS. IN RETURN I LEARN TO TRUST MYSELF.

Cheryl Sosnowski

I don't think about art when I'm working. **I try to think about life**.

Jean-Michel Basquiat

We all have to get
used to the fact that
there are no keys and
there are no locks.
Just revolving doors.

Maurizio Cattelan

UNLESS YOUR PAINTING GOES WRONG IT WILL BE NO GOOD.

Pablo Picasso

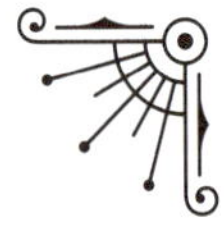

I think a painting is more like the real world if it's made out of the real world.

Robert Rauschenberg

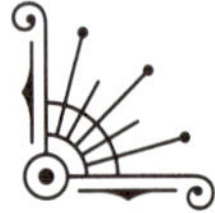

IF YOU GET TIRED, LEARN TO REST, NOT TO QUIT.

Banksy

I found I could say things with colour and shapes that I couldn't say any other way.

Georgia O'Keeffe

I am always doing what
I cannot do yet in order
to learn how to do it.

Vincent van Gogh

IT DOESN'T MATTER HOW THE PAINT IS PUT ON, AS LONG AS SOMETHING IS SAID.

Jackson Pollock

If I create from
the heart, nearly
everything works;
**if it's from the head,
almost nothing.**

Marc Chagall

I would like to paint the way a bird sings.

Claude Monet

NO ARTIST TOLERATES REALITY.

Friedrich Nietzsche

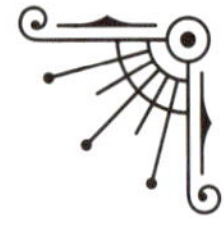

Do not worry about your originality. You could not get rid of it even if you wanted to.

Robert Henri

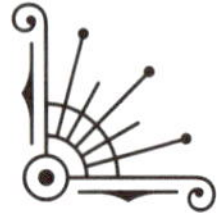

AN ARTIST CAN SHOW THINGS THAT OTHER PEOPLE ARE TERRIFIED OF EXPRESSING.

Louise Bourgeois

Have no fear of perfection
– you'll never reach it.

Salvador Dalí

If I knew what the picture was going to be like I wouldn't make it.

Cindy Sherman

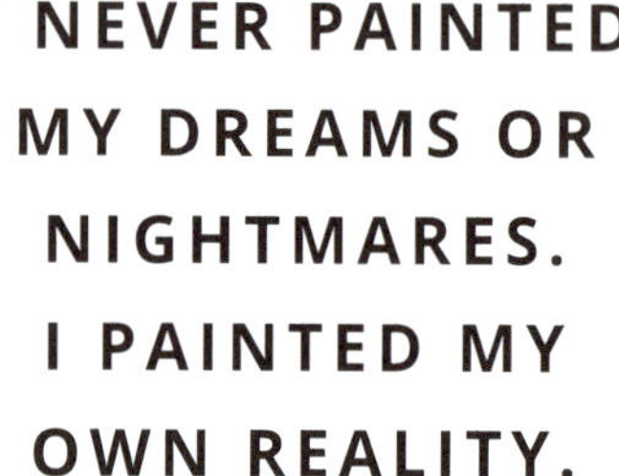

I NEVER PAINTED MY DREAMS OR NIGHTMARES. I PAINTED MY OWN REALITY.

Frida Kahlo

A painting that is well composed is **half finished.**

Pierre Bonnard

Art... it's about who we are, what happened to us and how our lives are affected.

Elizabeth Broun

ONE EYE SEES,
THE OTHER
FEELS.

Paul Klee

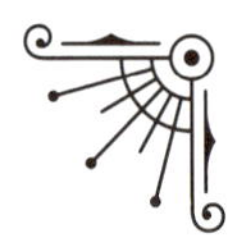

A painter should begin every canvas with a wash of black, because all things in nature are dark except where exposed by the light.

Leonardo da Vinci

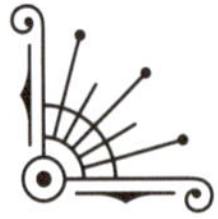

ART IS AN ESSENCE, A CENTRE.

Eva Hesse

Even though I collect and work with images in the studio they don't enter the work directly. Instead I'm trying to create my own language.

Julie Mehretu

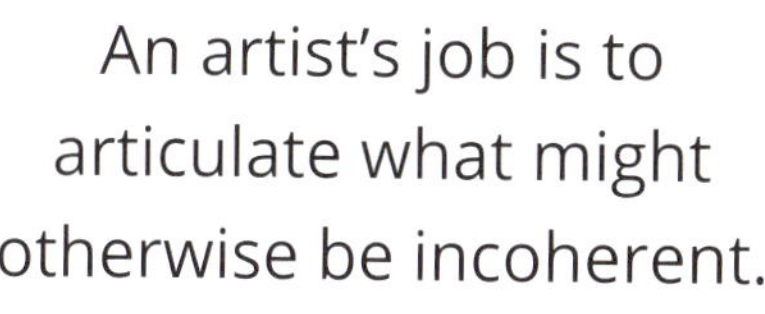

An artist's job is to articulate what might otherwise be incoherent.

Nancy Spero

THE MAIN THING IS TO BE MOVED, TO LOVE, TO HOPE, TO TREMBLE, TO LIVE.

Auguste Rodin

The job of the artist is always to **deepen the mystery.**

Francis Bacon

The longer you look at an object the more abstract it becomes, and, ironically, the more real.

Lucian Freud

THE GREAT ENEMY OF CREATIVITY IS FEAR.

Faith Ringgold

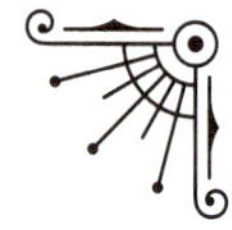

There is nothing worse than a sharp image of a fuzzy concept.

Ansel Adams

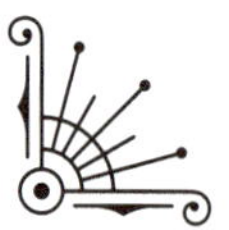

ART… EVOKES THE MYSTERY WITHOUT WHICH THE WORLD WOULD NOT EXIST.

René Magritte

Art is an adventure into an unknown world, which can only be explored by those willing to take the risks.

Mark Rothko

If people knew how hard I worked to get my mastery, it wouldn't seem so wonderful at all.

Michelangelo

I JUST WANTED TO FIND OUT WHERE THE BOUNDARIES WERE. I'VE FOUND THERE AREN'T ANY.

Damien Hirst

The essence of all beautiful art, **all great art, is gratitude.**

Friedrich Nietzsche

Painting is by nature a luminous language.

Robert Delaunay

NOTHING IS ART IF IT DOES NOT COME FROM NATURE.

Antoni Gaudí

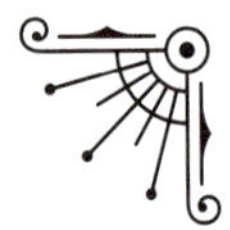

People discuss my art and pretend to understand as if it were necessary to understand, when it's simply necessary to love.

Claude Monet

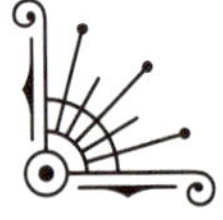

ONE MUST NOT BE AFRAID OF MAKING MISTAKES NOW AND THEN.

Vincent van Gogh

Good teaching is more a giving of right questions than a giving of right answers.

Josef Albers

Painting is a source of endless pleasure, but also of great anguish.

Balthus

THE REALITY IS THE PICTURE; IT IS MOST CERTAINLY NOT IN THE PICTURE.

Georg Baselitz

Artists, to my mind, are the **real architects of change.**

William S. Burroughs

The true method of knowledge is experiment.

William Blake

EVERY LINE
MEANS

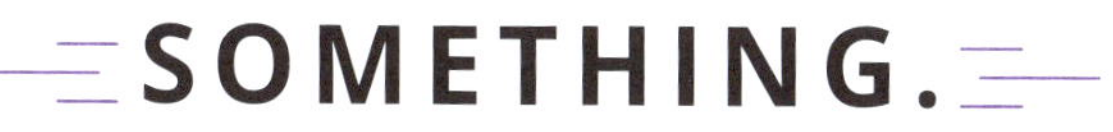

Jean-Michel Basquiat

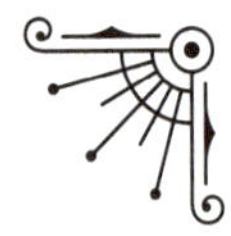

In art progress consists not in extension, but in the knowledge of its limits.

Georges Braque

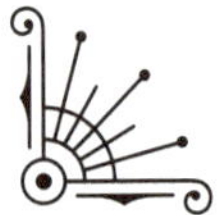

THE LOUVRE IS THE BOOK IN WHICH WE LEARN TO READ.

Paul Cézanne

Only love interests me,
and I am only in contact
with the things I love.

Marc Chagall

It is not enough to give signals. Things can only ever last if they have functioned as signs.

Enzo Cucchi

AN ARTIST'S EARLY WORK IS INEVITABLY MADE UP OF A MIXTURE OF TENDENCIES AND INTERESTS.

Bridget Riley

Where the spirit does not work with the hand **there is no art.**

Leonardo da Vinci

In a successful painting
everything is integral...
all the parts belong
to the whole.

Richard Diebenkorn

I DO NOT BELIEVE IN ART. I BELIEVE IN THE ARTIST.

Marcel Duchamp

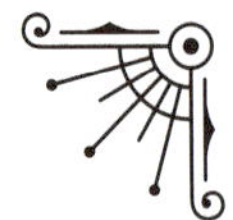

You have to systematically create confusion, it sets creativity free. Everything that is contradictory creates life.

Salvador Dalí

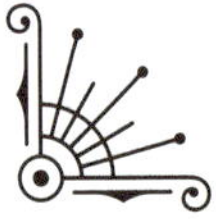

WHEN THERE'S ANYTHING TO STEAL, I STEAL.

Pablo Picasso

Choose only one master... Nature.

Rembrandt

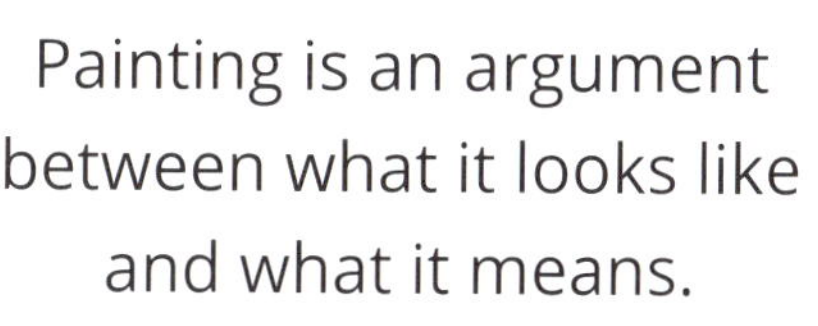

Painting is an argument between what it looks like and what it means.

Brett Whiteley

I TRY TO APPLY COLOURS LIKE WORDS THAT SHAPE POEMS, LIKE NOTES THAT SHAPE MUSIC.

Joan Miró

Painting is not very difficult when you don’t know how; but when you know, oh! **then, it’s another matter.**

Edgar Degas

An artist cannot fail; it is a success to be one.

Charles Horton Cooley

YOU INSTINCTIVELY LIKE WHAT YOU CAN'T DO.

Franz Kline

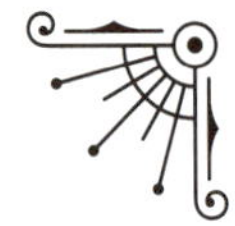

I work with pictures and words because they have the ability to determine who we are, what we want to be.

Barbara Kruger

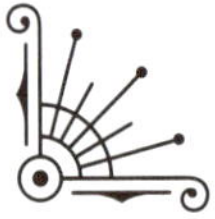

ART IS NEVER FINISHED, ONLY ABANDONED.

Leonardo da Vinci

What I expect from any work of art is that it surprises me, that it violates my customary valuations of things and offers me other, unexpected ones.

Jean Dubuffet

Every artist should be ahead of his time and behind in his rent.

Kinky Friedman

I ALWAYS SUSPECT AN ARTIST WHO IS SUCCESSFUL BEFORE HE IS DEAD.

John Murray Gibbon

Art enables us to find ourselves and lose ourselves **at the same time.**

Thomas Merton

To be an artist is to believe in life.

Henry Moore

I SHUT MY

EYES IN ORDER

TO SEE.

Paul Gauguin

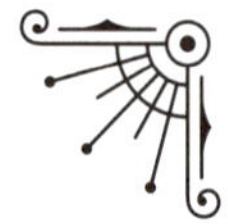

Controversy is part of the nature of art and creativity.

Yoko Ono

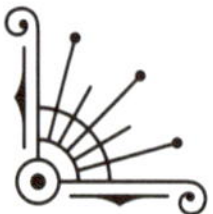

MY IDEAS ARE ALL THE SAME BUT LOOK DIFFERENT.

Maurizio Cattelan

He paints with his brains
and not with his hands.

Michelangelo

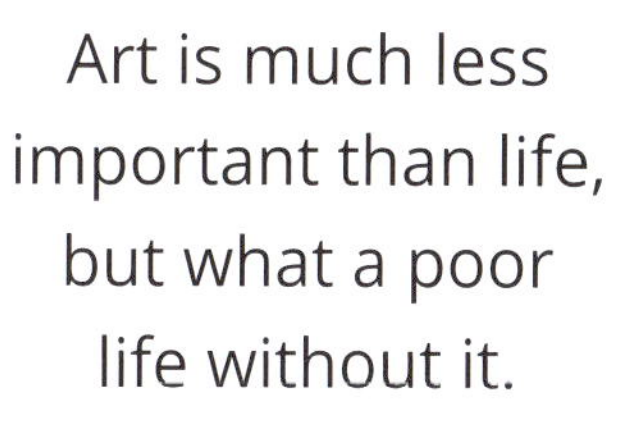

Art is much less important than life, but what a poor life without it.

Robert Motherwell

WHENEVER I AM EMBRACED BY LAND AND SEASCAPE I DRAW IDEAS FOR NEW SCULPTURES.

Barbara Hepworth

The artist who aims at perfection in everything **achieves it in nothing.**

Eugène Delacroix

Creativity is allowing yourself to make mistakes. Art is knowing which ones to keep.

Scott Adams

ART IS NOT A THING; IT IS A WAY.

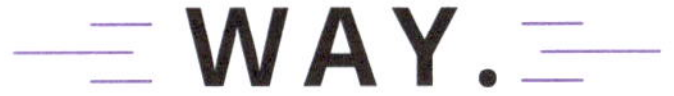

Elbert Hubbard

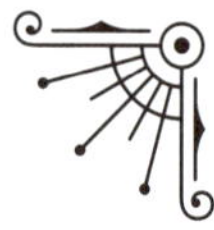

When I work, I work very fast, but preparing to work can take any length of time.

Cy Twombly

THIS WORLD IS BUT A CANVAS TO OUR IMAGINATION.

Henry David Thoreau

To be a truly conscientious artist, you have to look at what's not working and challenge it. You riff on things.

Kara Walker

Art is like a border
of flowers along the
course of civilisation.

Lincoln Steffens

A GREAT ARTIST IS ALWAYS BEFORE HIS TIME OR BEHIND IT.

George Moore

One must from time to time attempt things that are **beyond one's capacity.**

Pierre-Auguste Renoir

Blessed are they who see beautiful things in humble places where other people see nothing.

Camille Pissarro

ART IS EVERYWHERE, EXCEPT IT HAS TO PASS THROUGH A CREATIVE MIND.

Louise Nevelson

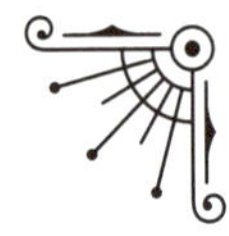

Only when he
no longer knows
what he is doing
does the painter
do good things.

Edgar Degas

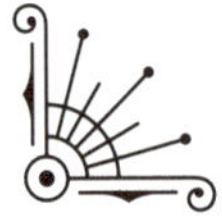

ART MUST BE AN EXPRESSION OF LOVE OR IT IS NOTHING.

Marc Chagall

Treat a work of art like a prince. Let it speak to you first.

Arthur Schopenhauer

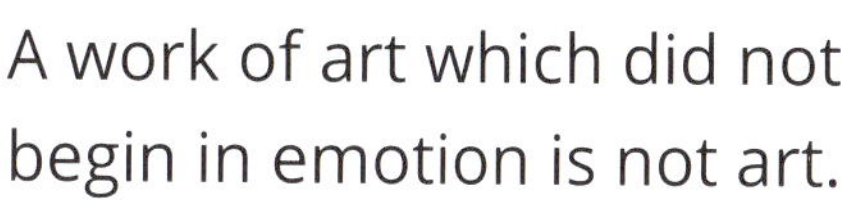

A work of art which did not begin in emotion is not art.

Paul Cézanne

IF I COULD SAY IT IN WORDS THERE WOULD BE NO REASON TO PAINT.

Edward Hopper

The position of the
artist is humble.
He is **essentially
a channel.**

Piet Mondrian

An artist is not paid
for his labour but
for his vision.

James McNeill Whistler

TO CREATE ONE’S OWN WORLD IN ANY OF THE ARTS TAKES COURAGE.

Georgia O’Keeffe

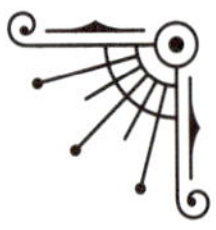

Art does not reproduce what we see. It makes us see.

Paul Klee

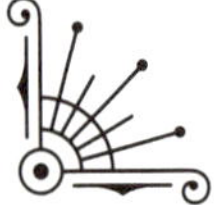

THE ONLY
TIME I FEEL
ALIVE IS WHEN
I'M PAINTING.

Vincent van Gogh

Painting completed my life.

Frida Kahlo

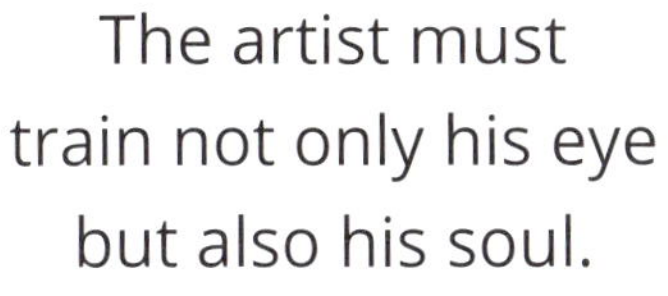

The artist must
train not only his eye
but also his soul.

Wassily Kandinsky

IN ART ONE
IS EITHER A
PLAGIARIST OR A
REVOLUTIONARY.

Paul Gauguin

Let the form of an object be what it may – light, shade, and perspective will always **make it beautiful.**

John Constable

I saw the angel in the marble and carved until I set him free.

Michelangelo

ART IS ABOUT MYSTERY.

Marisol

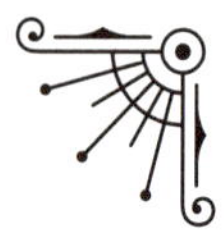

It's on the strength of observation and reflection that one finds a way. So we must dig and delve unceasingly.

Claude Monet

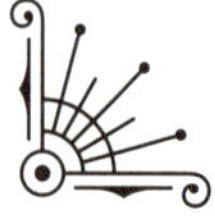

TRUE ART IS CHARACTERISED BY AN IRRESISTIBLE URGE IN THE CREATIVE ARTIST.

Albert Einstein

Those who do not want
to imitate anything,
produce nothing.

Salvador Dalí

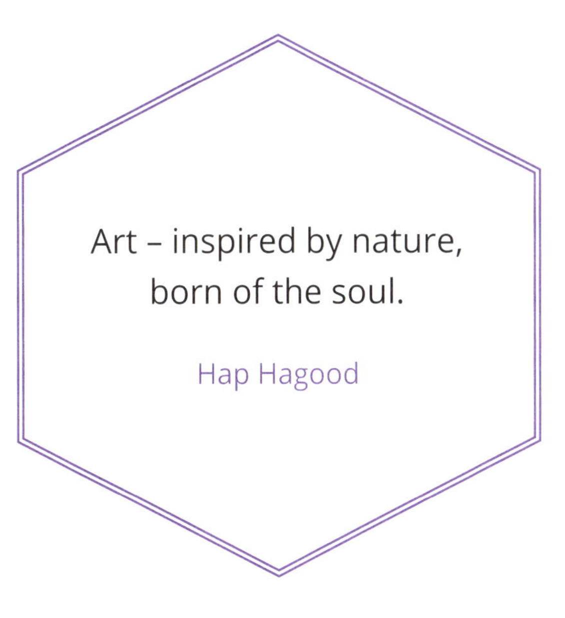
Art – inspired by nature,
born of the soul.
Hap Hagood

IT'S AMAZING THAT YOU CAN WIN THE TURNER PRIZE WITH AN E IN A-LEVEL ART, A TWISTED IMAGINATION AND A CHAINSAW.

Damien Hirst

Creativity is the art of **concealing your sources.**

C. E. M. Joad

The moment you cheat for the sake of beauty, you know you are an artist.

David Hockney

GOOD ART
IS NOT WHAT
IT LOOKS LIKE,
BUT WHAT
IT DOES
TO US.

Roy Adzak

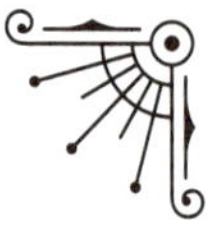

Art, n. This word has no definition.

Ambrose Bierce

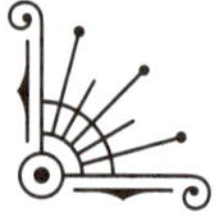

ART IS NOT A PASTIME BUT A PRIESTHOOD.

Jean Cocteau

Works of art are
landscapes of the mind.

Ted Godwin

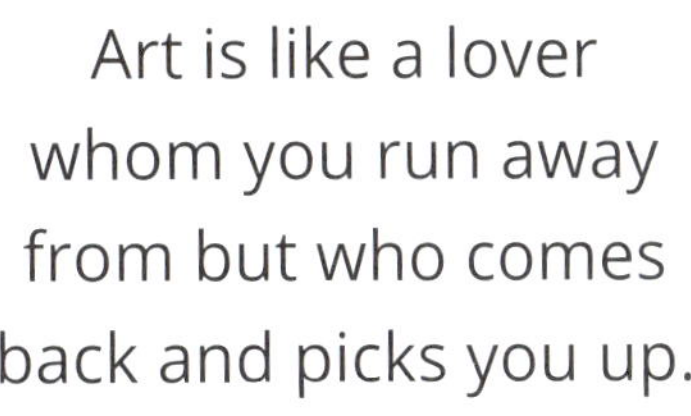

Art is like a lover whom you run away from but who comes back and picks you up.

Tracey Emin

ART SHOULD CREATE AN EXPERIENCE.

Eric Fischl

A work of art is the trace of **a magnificent struggle.**

Robert Henri

No amount of skilful invention can replace the essential element of imagination.

Edward Hopper

ART ISN'T PAINT; IT'S LOVE.

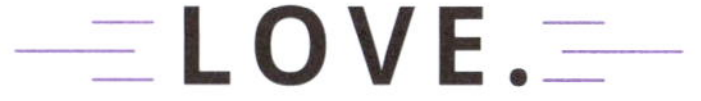

Philip Hicken

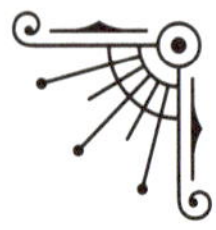

Art is a line around your thoughts.

Gustav Klimt

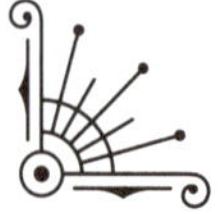

WITHOUT EMOTION, ART IS LIFELESS; WITHOUT INTELLECT ART IS SHAPELESS.

Charles Johnson

Art is not what you see, but what you make others see.

Edgar Degas

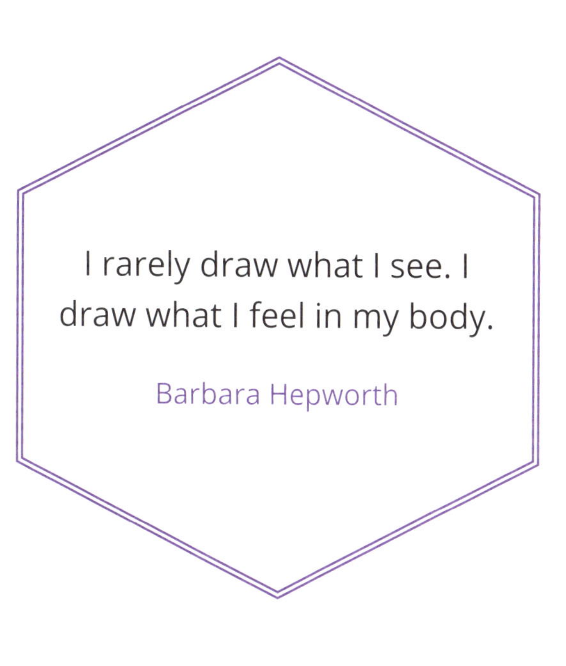

I rarely draw what I see. I draw what I feel in my body.

Barbara Hepworth

ART SHOULD BE SOMETHING LIKE A GOOD ARMCHAIR IN WHICH TO REST FROM PHYSICAL FATIGUE.

Henri Matisse

The artist should open the eyes of the viewer to overlooked beauty that is sometimes **right in front of us.**

Kenn Backhaus

Art is the demonstration that the ordinary is extraordinary.

Amédée Ozenfant

ART IS THE ONLY MEANS BY WHICH ONE SOUL CAN TRULY TOUCH ANOTHER.

Curtis Verdun

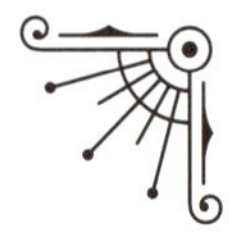

Fine art is that in which the hand, the head, and the heart of man go together.

John Ruskin

ACTION IS THE FOUNDATIONAL KEY TO ALL SUCCESS.

Pablo Picasso

Art happens all the time, everywhere. All we have to do is to keep our minds open.

Jacek Tylicki

The artist that paints every tiny little detail is an artist with nothing better to do.

Sam Adoquei

EVERY MAN IS AN ARTIST.

Joseph Beuys

I would like to show the world today as an ant sees it and tomorrow **as the moon sees it.**

Hannah Höch

Art is not a matter
of life and death.
It's much more
important than that.

Andrew Mercer

COLOUR IS
MY DAY-LONG
OBSESSION,
JOY AND
TORMENT.

Claude Monet

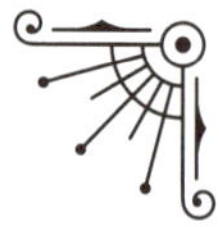

Painting is no problem. The problem is what to do when you're not painting.

Jackson Pollock

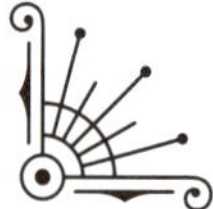

IN MY INNER SOUL ART AND LIFE ARE INSEPARABLE.

Eva Hesse

The mind is the limit. As long as the mind can envision the fact that you can do something, you can do it, as long as you really believe 100 per cent.

David Hockney

The object of art is
not to reproduce reality,
but to create a reality of
the same intensity.

Alberto Giacometti

ALL THAT IS NECESSARY TO PAINT WELL IS TO BE SINCERE.

Maurice Denis

Art is that which comes to a man, and stands between himself and an implacable witness – **the work.**

Eduardo Chillida

What I try to give form
to is the subjective
experiences of living
behind our faces.

Antony Gormley

THE ARTIST'S JOB IS TO BE A WITNESS TO HIS TIME IN HISTORY.

Robert Rauschenberg

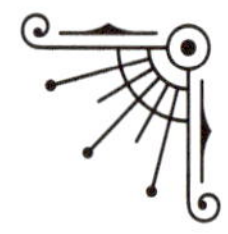

Draw your pleasure,
paint your pleasure,
and express your
pleasure strongly.

Pierre Bonnard

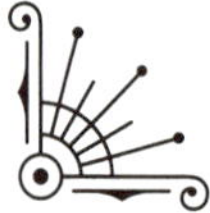

GREAT ART PICKS UP WHERE NATURE ENDS.

Marc Chagall

Art is a fruit that grows in man, like a fruit on a plant, or a child in its mother's womb.

Jean Arp

What does it matter how you do it? Paint it with a shovel if you can't get your effect any other way.

John Everett Millais

A GOOD ARTIST HAS LESS TIME THAN IDEAS.

Martin Kippenberger

An artist should never be a prisoner of himself, prisoner of style, prisoner of reputation, **prisoner of success**.

Henri Matisse

It took me four years
to paint like Raphael,
but a lifetime to
paint like a child.

Pablo Picasso

ART IS THE JOURNEY OF A FREE SOUL.

Alev Oguz

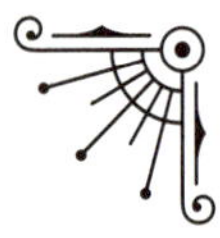

Whether you succeed or not is irrelevant, there is no such thing. Making your unknown known is the important thing.

Georgia O'Keeffe

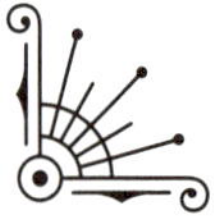

I PAINT FLOWERS SO THEY WILL NOT DIE.

Frida Kahlo

Art is anything you can get away with.

Marshall McLuhan

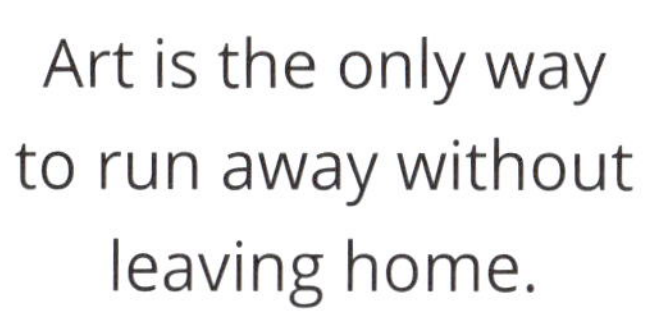

Art is the only way
to run away without
leaving home.

Twyla Tharp